Republicans Can Win

By Jon Ivy

ISBN: 9798328327985

First Edition Printed: 2019

Jon Ivy, Republicans Can Win
140 B St, # 5-179
Davis, CA 95616

jon@CARepublicans.org
www.CARepublicans.org

Contents

Preface

The purpose of this booklet, as referenced in the title, is to provide a platform to build a new Republican Party that can win elections here in California and nationally.

Namely, **Republicans Can Win** by adopting a progressive platform and running campaigns on progressive ideas. And this platform represents some of the best progressive ideas that the author could think of.

The book is divided into sections, with one section for each of the eight platform "planks."

At the end of the booklet is an index which lists some individual political issues and gives page numbers to where each topic is discussed. Going to the index first is a perfectly acceptable place to start. But the introduction that follows this preface can also give you some great context for the platform as a whole.

Introduction

The Republican Party of today is almost unrecognizable from what it looked like during the time of Abraham Lincoln in the 19th century.

Likewise, President Lincoln thought similarly about the Democratic Party of his day and how far it had moved from its Jeffersonian roots. Lincoln had the following to say in response to an invitation to celebrate Jefferson's memorial in Boston leading up to the 1860 election:

"Bearing in mind that about seventy years ago, two great political parties were first formed in this country, that Thomas Jefferson was the head of one of them, and Boston the head-quarters of the other, it is both curious and interesting that those supposed to descend politically from the party opposed to Jefferson should now be celebrating his birthday in their own

original seat of empire, while those claiming political descent from him have nearly ceased to breathe his name everywhere.

"Remembering too, that the Jefferson party were formed upon its supposed superior devotion to the personal rights of men, holding the rights of property to be secondary only, and greatly inferior, and then assuming that the so-called democracy of to-day, are the Jefferson, and their opponents, the anti-Jefferson parties, it will be equally interesting to note how completely the two have changed hands as to the principle upon which they were originally supposed to be divided.

"The democracy of to-day hold the liberty of one man to be absolutely nothing, when in conflict with another man's right of property. Republicans, on the contrary, are for both the man and the dollar; but in cases of conflict, the man before the dollar." [1]

There are lessons we can learn from President Lincoln and similar Republican figures of the 19th, 20th, and 21st centuries. They can show us how progressive ideals have shaped our nation and our communities. They can instill upon us the type of patriotism that demands hard work, optimism, and a desire for universal justice. That kind of patriotism demands ever-more work from our fellow citizens, our government, and ourselves.

It is hard to find a Republican Party leader today who matches the progressive spirit of Lincoln. And that is a shame. Our country has two major parties, and both should be led by people who inspire greatness. For that to be true, both parties are in need of major reforms.

One of these parties, the Democratic Party, has felt a recent surge of liberal progressive sentiment. While the party is still largely controlled by rich corporate interests, people

---

[1] Lincoln, Abraham. Letter to Henry L. Pierce and others, 1859

who want to reform the Democratic Party have taken to the streets, have taken to the capital offices, and have taken to the ballot box. Organizations, like Indivisible and Justice Democrats are starting to win major support among Democratic voters. It's really starting to look like there's hope for real progressive change in the Democratic Party.

The other of these two parties, the Republican Party, has recently been taken over by right-wing white nationalists. As a result, our nation has as its President an out and open white nationalist, an oligarch, a fascist. And he, along with the Republicans in Congress, have started to tear our country apart. They've given billions of dollars away to their rich friends, locked children in cages and camps, and are supporting genocidal policies globally.

We need to completely transform the Republican Party in our country. There shouldn't be a major political party in our country that accepts and promotes racism, fascism, and Nazism. There shouldn't be a major political party in our country that provides support for rich oligarchs, endless war, and cruel domestic policies.

And in transforming the Republican Party with a progressive political revolution, we can also defeat the corporate-backed Democrats. A progressive Republican will always have an advantage over their Democratic rival. The heart and soul of the Republican Party and the progressive ideals that it was formed with can beat corporate interests in every election.

Republicans can win against Democrats that don't care about working-class people. Republicans can win on a progressive platform. Republicans can win if their candidates are good, moral people opposed to fascism, homophobia, xenophobia, racism, and white nationalism. And so, the Republican Party needs a new progressive platform that can rally support, build political will, and change our nation:

"Our economy is rigged and we need to fix it. We need to protect ourselves and our families from climate change. Republicans don't just resist fascism, racism, and Nazism; we defeat those evils wherever they're found. Competition among businesses is essential to a free market. Universal healthcare is a moral imperative. Public education is essential to a working democracy. We must expand opportunities for voting, get money out of politics, and guarantee a right to vote to all Americans. It is our duty to teach good civic engagement to our children."

Our economy is rigged and we need to fix it.

Abraham Lincoln gave many speeches outlining what we would call the American Dream. A line from one such speech reads:

"We proposed to give all a chance; and we expected the weak to grow stronger, the ignorant, wiser; and all better, and happier together." [2]

The American Dream is one of opportunity and equality. As one of the richest nations on Earth, the United States is a place of immense opportunity. However, opportunity should not be held in just a few hands. **Inequality shortchanges the American Dream.** Equality and opportunity are both needed in

---

[2] Lincoln, Abraham. Speech fragment on slavery and American government, 1857.

order to fulfill our ideals. The American Dream is not just for the few; it is for the many. *E pluribus unum.*[3]

The wealth gap and income inequality between the rich and poor is greater now than at any previous time in our nation's history. The richest 0.00025 percent of the American population now owns more wealth than the 150,000,000 adults in the bottom 60 percent.[4] The nationwide poverty-rate is 12.9% for people living in cities and 16.4% for people living outside of cities.[5] There is a huge divide between the working-class people and the trust-fund-elites throughout the United States.

The Republican Party and Democratic Party leadership have both consistently ignored the needs of the working-class people in our nation. While the rich are enjoying the lowest tax rates in American history,[6] the rest of us are working longer hours for less money.[7]

---

[3] Out of many, one. (US Motto)

[4] Johnson, Jake. "Study Shows Richest 0.00025 Percent Owns More Wealth Than Bottom 150 Million Americans." Feb. 2019. Truthout. Accessed 19 Jul. 2019. https://truthout.org/articles/study-shows-richest-0-00025-owns-more-wealth-than-bottom-150-million-americans/

[5] USDA ERS – Rural Poverty & Wealth. Accessed 19 July 2019. https://www.ers.usda.gov/topics/rural-economy-population/rural-poverty-well-being/

[6] See Novak, Janet. "The Very Rich Are Different–They Pay A Lower Tax Rate", 2010. Forbes Online. Accessed July 19, 2019. https://www.forbes.com/sites/janetnovack/2010/09/23/the-very-rich-are-different-they-pay-a-lower-tax-rate/

[7] See Carmichael, Sarah Green. "Millennials Are Actually Workaholics, According to Research", 2016. Harvard

The American Dream is impossible in a system where no matter how hard one works, there is no path to success. Government's role can be found in helping to ensure a system where every American has the opportunity to succeed in life. This ideal has been the banner of the Republican party since the leadership of Lincoln, but recent Republican politicians have lost their way. **The economy is doing great for Wall Street; but it's not doing anything for the rest of us.**

Now, in place of the American Dream we have the Big Lie – people born rich pretending that they worked hard to get their riches and that our being born poor is some kind of "moral failing."

If there's one thing that should define the Republican Party, it should be our belief in the righteousness of the working class. **Working for a living and working for the betterment of all people are not moral failings.** To quote Abraham Lincoln:

"I hold that while man exists, it is his duty to improve not only his own condition, but to assist in ameliorating mankind; and therefore, without entering upon the details of the question, I will simply say, that I am for those means which will give the greatest good to the greatest number." [8]

Business Review. Accessed July 19, 2019. https://hbr.org/2016/08/millennials-are-actually-workaholics-according-to-research

[8] Lincoln, Abraham. Speech to Germans at Cincinnati, Ohio, 1861.

The Republican Party was the first to enact a progressive income tax system in the United States.[9] Before Lincoln's "internal" tax, government revenues consisted solely of "external" taxes such as the Tariff along with money from the sale of public lands. But such "external" taxes and land sales quickly became insufficient for our growing and industrializing nation.

The transformation of the American economy into its modern form owes its success to idealistic views of people like Abraham Lincoln, the progressive Whig and later progressive Republican, and others like him. It wasn't until the New Deal that the Democratic Party fully took up the mantle of progressive politics. And it wasn't until President Reagan was in office that the Republican Party completely shed its progressive roots and became a shell of its former glory.

Reagan talked about "starving the beast" and modern Republicans have talked about making government so small you could "drown it in the bathtub."[10] But we're the ones that are starving. And it's our heads those right-wing politicians in both parties are holding under water. The thing they're drowning is the American Dream.

***

---

[9] See "Lincoln imposes first federal income tax", 2009. History.com Editors. Accessed July 19, 2019. https://www.history.com/this-day-in-history/lincoln-imposes-first-federal-income-tax

[10] "I don't want to abolish government. I simply want to reduce it to the size where I can drag it into the bathroom and drown it in the bathtub." Norquist, Grover. Interview on NPR's Morning Edition, May 25, 2001.

Tax rates should reflect the wealth of our nation. With a slight increase to taxes on our richest citizens and richest corporations, we would raise enough money to do great things, important things, and necessary things. Those rich people will spend a great deal of money on advertisements and television programs designed to convince the poor and middle-class Americans that taxes are evil.

The greatest evil facing America today is that of rich people not paying their fair share. They're getting dividends from the economy without making the investment. They're cheating all of us and using the government to help. And as long as we have a government, it'd be better if that government was on our side. **Americans need a government that does its job.**

We need a government that provides a platform to stand on for people lifting themselves out of poverty. The federal Earned Income Tax Credit (EITC) should be expanded to provide more support for both families and individual workers whether or not they have children. Workers should be given the opportunity to rise in the world, and the EITC can help eliminate some of the barriers they face.

To ensure that America is a place with a working market for labor, a market that works both for businesses and works for the employees, our government should enact a Jobs Guarantee. Establishment of a jobs guarantee at the federal level would help create a system where we look nationally at unemployment and ensure that any labor market failures are dealt with as a country. There shouldn't be poor states and rich states, poor counties and rich counties, when it comes to the availability of work for those who want it.

As technology takes over whole industries and puts many workers out of work, we need to provide a system where losing your job doesn't result in you falling into poverty. One way to help improve the labor market's fluidity in changing times is to establish programs for a **Guaranteed Basic Income**. Such a Basic Income would provide a safety net for the workers, and would also help to ensure the system of hiring and firing, of finding the right worker for the right job, would be more efficient and effective. It's a lot easier to get an employee working for you that wants your company to succeed if they have a good choice of where and how to work. **The job you choose is the job you do well.**

Caring about American jobs doesn't mean cutting ourselves off from the world market. Trade between nations can lead to better conditions for businesses, workers, and consumers on both sides of the border. However, exploitative relationships with other countries can deprive America of jobs and opportunities for entrepreneurship, while placing foreign populations into unsafe working conditions with low pay.

Governments and large corporations have the responsibility to ensure the world market is stable and fair. We need to make sure that the same standards for labor, environment, and human rights that apply in the U.S. to American companies apply to our foreign trading partners and foreign-operating corporations. Fair rules that apply globally can help ensure working conditions and business conditions meet our policy goals here and abroad.

Included in any regulatory standard for labor conditions, we must address the wage gap between men and women, both in urban and rural areas of our country.[11] Whatever the causes for the pay gap, the solutions should focus on ensuring women have the same opportunities as men, are paid the same for the same work, and are provided with a work environment free from sexism and misogyny. To this end, it is essential that Congress pushes the states to adopt the **Equal Rights Amendment**, and provide for equal rights to men and women under our federal constitution.

---

[11] See Robbins, Katherine Gallagher, et al. "The Gender Wage Gap Among Rural Workers", 2018. Center for American Progress.

We need to protect ourselves and our families from climate change.

Climate change is the number one national security threat facing the United States of America. Our response to climate change will require a mobilization of people and resources that rivals any we've undertaken before. In line with our economic vision, the United States should adopt the framework of the Green New Deal.[12]

The greatest failure in America's political discourse over the last forty years has been the debate over climate change. Debate is an important part of Democracy. But this debate has

------

[12] See H.Res.109 – Recognizing the duty of the Federal Government to create a Green New Deal. 116th Congress.

been a failure. Instead of debating the best course of action to help protect humanity and prevent further destruction from climate change, we've been debating the very existence of the phenomena. We've entertained a debate with the most anti-science, anti-thought group of people to ever walk the Earth. And that must stop.

We must start debating solutions that we should have started debating 40 years ago. **We must start figuring out the best way forward on climate action.** That is the great debate we must have. And one group of people we cannot allow on the debate stage is that same group that denied the existence of human-caused climate change. Those people have no business speaking in public or pretending to lead our party or our nation.

One step we can take as a nation in our fight against climate change is to end our reliance on fossil fuels and switch to renewable energy production. This change has already started with investment in renewable energy throughout the United States. However, even with our current investments in renewable energy, coal and natural gas combined provided 63% of electricity generation for America in 2018.[13] We simply aren't moving fast enough away from fossil fuel reliance. **We must take action to dramatically expand and upgrade renewable power sources.**

***

---

[13] Source: U.S. Energy Information Administration, Short-Term Energy Outlook, January 2019. Accessed 19 July 2019. https://www.eia.gov/todayinenergy/detail.php?id=38053

An international framework of human rights should include the principles of climate justice and environmental justice. Climate change has a disproportionate effect on communities of color, working-class communities, and low-income communities throughout the United States and around the world. The Green New Deal not only addresses the impact of climate injustice on these communities, but it also seeks to ensure these communities are centered in the fight against climate change. The right to clean water, without fear of lead-filled pipes or toxic runoff, should be guaranteed to all Americans. **No community should go without water.**

***

Dealing with the effects of climate change and working to prevent further damage to our nation requires us to reevaluate our national security priorities, objectives, and preparations. We cannot afford to waste billions of dollars supporting a military posture that acts as welfare for weapons manufactures. We don't need another fighter jet.[14] We don't need weapons manufactures acting as advisers to military leaders. **The market should not dictate when we go to war.**

It is time to end the "Endless War", bring our troops home, and train them to tackle the coming humanitarian crisis that climate change will bring. We need rescue workers, engineers,

---

[14] See Hughes, Michael P. "What Went Wrong with the F-35, Lockheed Martin's Joint Strike Fighter?", 2017. Scientific American. Accessed 19 July 2019.
https://www.scientificamerican.com/article/what-went-wrong-with-the-f-35-lockheed-martins-joint-strike-fighter/

and transportation experts to make sure that when a storm, tornado, fire, or earthquake hits, we can react. It's called the "Department of Defense" and its focus should be on defending the people and property within the United States from threats like climate change.

Reforming military spending doesn't mean putting an industry out of work. If a factory can make bombs, then it can make tools for digging septic systems. If a factory can make parts for a fighter jet, then it can make parts for water filtration systems. If we're going to spend the money,[15] let's spend it on things we can actually use. **We need to plan for peace and spend for it.**

____

[15] We spend about 690 billion dollars a year on our military. See the National Defense Budget Estimates for FY 2020. U.S. Comptroller. Accessed 19 July 2019. https://comptroller.defense.gov/Portals/45/Documents/def budget/fy2020/FY20_Green_Book.pdf

Republicans don't just resist fascism, racism, and Nazism; we defeat those evils wherever they're found.

As former Secretary of State Colin Powell said in 2013,

"In my lifetime, over a long career in public life, you know, I've been refused access to restaurants where I couldn't eat, even though I just came back from Vietnam: 'We can't give you a hamburger, come back some other time,'... And I did, right after the Civil Rights Act of 1964 was passed, I went right back to that same place and got my hamburger, and they were more than happy to serve me now. It removed a cross from their back, but

we're not there yet. We're not there yet. And so we've got to keep working on it." [16]

The Republican Party has not always been the primary political home of racists and white supremacists.[17] The party was formed to end slavery in America.[18] And for more than a century, the Republican Party stood for equality, opportunity, and free enterprise.[19] Even while the country still suffered under segregation and Jim Crow laws, President Dwight D. Eisenhower, as expressed in his 1961 State of the Union address, celebrated his party's work on civil rights:

This pioneering work in civil rights must go on. Not only because discrimination is morally wrong, but also because its impact is more than national—it is world-wide.[20]

---

[16] Jamieson, Dave. "Colin Powell: Voter ID Laws Will 'Backfire' for Republicans", 2013. HuffPost Online. Accessed 19 July 2019. https://www.huffpost.com/entry/colin-powell-voter-id-laws-backfire_n_3813092.

[17] Though, that's certainly what it's become. See Harriot, Michael. "How the Republican Party Became The Party of Racism", 2018. The Root. Accessed 19 July 2019. https://www.theroot.com/how-the-republican-party-became-the-party-of-racism-1827779221.

[18] Prokop, Andrew. "See How Republicans went from the party of Lincoln to the party of Trump, in 13 maps", 2016. Vox. https://www.vox.com/2016/7/20/12148750/republican-party-trump-lincoln.

[19] See Shesol, Jeff. "Do Conservatives Own 'Opportunity'?", 2014. The New Yorker. https://www.newyorker.com/news/news-desk/do-conservatives-own-opportunity.

[20] Eisenhower, Dwight D. State of the Union Address, 1961. Accessed 19 July 2019.

Even before that, in 1940, the Republican Party chose as their nominee for President a reluctant interventionist named Wendell Willkie.[21] Like many Republicans and many war veterans of then and now, Willkie had been to war and didn't like the idea of America joining another one.[22] But by 1940, the evil of the Nazis and the evil of doing nothing was clear to Willkie and many Americans.[23]

Willkie made a point of not just being free from racism in his ideology and actions, but he also wasn't quiet about his anti-racist stances. He would often tell the story of how he once wrote in response to the Ku Klux Klan seeking his support:

"The Klan can go to hell."

---

    https://www.infoplease.com/homework-help/us-documents/dwight-d-eisenhower-january-12-1961.

[21] Willkie, Wendell L. II. "My Grandfather Was a Republican Nominee Who Put Country First", 2018. The Atlantic. Accessed 19 July 2019. https://www.theatlantic.com/ideas/archive/2018/10/wendell-willkie/572290/.

[22] See Ibid.

[23] "The story of the barbarous and worse than medieval persecution of the Jews—a race that has done so much to improve the culture of these countries and our own—is the most tragic in human history." Willkie, Wendell. Address Accepting the Presidential Nomination in Elwood, Indiana, 1940. Accessed 19 July 2019. https://www.presidency.ucsb.edu/documents/address-accepting-the-presidential-nomination-elwood-indiana.

After America's entry into World War II, Willkie would go around America spreading support for internationalism and the war effort. In one particularly poignant speech given in a small town in Illinois, he spoke of the burning of the town of Lidice[24] in what was then Czechoslovakia by Nazi forces:

"I look about me here, and I can see in the distance the black smoke of steel factories, swarming with American workers of all bloods and races. No contrast could be greater than the peaceful Lidice the Nazis thought they had destroyed, and this Illinois country, alive with factories in which the arms of victory are being forged. But I tell you that the two are related. For while such deeds as Lidice are done in another country, we cannot rest until we are sure that they will never be done in our own." [25]

While many Republican politicians today open their arms and the party to the far-right, to literal Nazis, and to white racists, nationalists, and supremacists, this must change. We cannot be the party of fascism, xenophobia, and racism. We cannot be a country that allows for such groups to thrive and exert political power. We didn't lose to the Nazis in the 20th century, and we should not be losing to them in the 21st. Republicans have a moral duty to fight these evils and to win that fight. **Republicans can win**.

***

---

[24] See "History of Lidice Village". Pamatnik Lidice. Accessed 24 July 2019. http://www.lidice-memorial.cz/en/memorial/memorial-and-reverent-area/history-of-the-village-lidice/.

[25] Willkie, Wendell. Eulogy of Lidice, 1942. Illinois. Accessed 19 July 2019. http://www.speeches-usa.com/Transcripts/wendell_wilkie-eulogy.html.

Another Republican, Marvin Liebman, wrote in 1992 that within the Republican Party he had begun to "feel like a Jew in Germany in 1934 who had chosen to remain silent, hoping to be able to stay invisible as he watched the beginning of the Holocaust."[26] Liebman was World War II veteran, a fundraiser and organizer for conservative causes, and a member of the Republican party for decades. Toward the end of his life, he became an outspoken advocate for gay rights and inclusion, coming out to the public as a gay man himself.

In the 1980's, he helped found the Log Cabin Republicans, an advocacy group within the Republican Party supporting LGBTQA+ rights. In the 90's, Liebman decided to leave the Republican Party. "The only identity of which I am absolutely certain," he said, "is that I am a homosexual in a country that has little patience with us."

The United States of America, and both of the two major parties, should be a place where different identities are welcomed.

What Liebman would have politely called the Religious Right, we now call fascists, homophobes, con-artists, and charlatans. From the 80's to today, they have taken a stranglehold over the Republican Party and over the United States government.

It should be a sincere priority of any Republican leader to defeat these evil men, cast them out from our party, and end their role in our government. **Every person, regardless of their gender or sexual orientation, should be welcome in our**

---

[26] Liebman, Marvin. Coming Out Conservative. 13. Chronicle Books: 1992.

society. No citizen of the United States of America should be made a second-class citizen in favor of a fake-morality that pretends differences are sins. LGBTQA+ identities should be protected under federal hate crime statutes and should also be protected from employment discrimination. **Our laws should reflect our moral values.**

***

Systemic reform is the most important weapon we have against racism. From over 400 years of slavery to the failures of reconstruction, from the Jim Crow South to redlining, our nation has a shameful history of systemic racism. Today we can see the effects of racist policies on mass incarceration, militarized police forces, and continued segregation along racial classifications throughout our country. Fighting racism means reforming the systems that propagate racism.

And while we are still working on how to treat the citizens we have; we must also do better in our treatment of immigrants. No one who approaches our border should be put in a cage. **We must say "never again" to concentration camps, to Nazism, to fascism, and to genocide.** We don't just need immigration reform for business reasons, which we do;[27] we don't just need immigration reform for societal reasons, which

---

[27] See Semotiuk, Andy J. "How Immigration Reform Could Help An Aging, Indebted America", 2018. Forbes. Accessed 19 July 2019.
https://www.forbes.com/sites/andyjsemotiuk/2018/07/25/how-immigration-reform-could-help-an-aging-indebted-america/#2c94bf3a4bff.

we do;[28] we need immigration reform as a basic prerequisite for calling ourselves a decent society. **No country has the right to exist; a nation is a responsibility.** And we have been failing in our responsibility.

Anyone who has lived in our nation and plans to call it home must be provided a path to citizenship. The current legal ways to immigrate to the United States are onerous, unfair, racist, and represent a system that is antithetical to the American way of doing things. **We are a nation of immigrants; we should be welcoming new immigrants.** We call ourselves "Americans;" we should at least provide a safe haven for American refugees. The crisis that our foreign policy mistakes have created in central America makes our immigration stance all the more evil and sadistic. We're locking up people who are fleeing the violence and poverty that we have created. That must end. Putting so many people in jail must end at the border, and it must end in our cities and our towns, as well.

***

We must make serious efforts toward criminal justice reform. We must end the era of mass incarceration, outlaw private for-profit prisons, and end race-based policing nationwide. As of 2016, 2.3 million people were imprisoned in

---

[28] See Gomez, Jose H. "The Moral Urgency of Immigration Reform", 2016. CNN Opinion. Accessed 19 July 2019. https://www.cnn.com/2016/01/27/politics/gomez-immigration-column/index.html.

the United States.[29] According to the U.S. Bureau of Justice Statistics, over 40 percent of those incarcerated are African American, even though African Americans only represent 13 percent of the nation's population.[30] This racial divide in our prison population points to systemic problems in policing and prosecutions, and it also points to systemic economic inequality.

We also need to take on reforms that help protect innocent people from wrongful incarceration, eliminate profit-driven policies, and tackle systemic injustices. We can end money bail in our nation and ensure that whether an innocent person spends a year in jail has nothing to do with how rich they are.[31] We can end the militarization of our police forces, ensuring that police officers are trained to de-escalate violent situations instead of resorting to violence themselves. And we can implement better gun regulation and control to ensure that neither police officers or the people they serve have to live in fear of gun violence. This means going after the gun manufactures, their lobbyists, their advertising, and their infiltration of our public agencies with tough laws that leave no middle ground.

---

[29] Sawyer, Wendy; Wagner, Peter. "Mass Incarceration: The Whole Pie 2019". Prison Policy Initiative. Accessed 19 July 2019. https://www.prisonpolicy.org/reports/pie2019.html.

[30] Carson, E. Ann. "Prisoners in 2013". Bureau of Justice Statistics. Accessed 19 July 2019. https://www.bjs.gov/content/pub/pdf/p13.pdf.

[31] See Wykstra, Stephanie. "Bail reform, which could save millions of unconvicted people from jail, explained", 2018. Vox. Accessed 19 July 2019. https://www.vox.com/future-perfect/2018/10/17/17955306/bail-reform-criminal-justice-inequality.

Effective police reform will also require major changes to how we view and use our police forces. We should not be spending so much effort on investigating property crimes or drug-related crimes; our focus should not be on policing the poorest individuals the most. We have plenty of laws on the books that need enforcement, such as laws against public corruption, laws against fraudulent business practices, and laws against domestic terrorism. Our Federal Bureau of Investigations should be mainly focused on white-collar crime, public corruption investigations, and enforcement of civil rights protections. Their budget, organization, and policy directives should be realigned to address the crimes that rich people perpetuate against the poor. **Instead of just one, there should be a thousand "Robert Mueller" style investigations into public corruption of our government offices.** No one who is stealing millions of dollars from the American people should sleep soundly at night.

We must end the failed War on Drugs. We must end marijuana prohibition and change federal law to allow for state marijuana legalization. According to the ACLU's analysis, marijuana arrests now account for over half of all drug arrests in the United States.[32] Of the 8.2 million marijuana arrests between 2001 and 2010, 88% were for simply having marijuana.[33] Nationwide, the arrest data revealed one consistent trend: significant racial bias. Despite roughly equal

---

[32] "Marijuana Arrests by the Numbers." American Civil Liberties Union. Accessed 19 July 2019.
https://www.aclu.org/gallery/marijuana-arrests-numbers.
[33] Ibid.

usage rates, African Americans are 3.73 times more likely than whites to be arrested for marijuana.[34]

Drug use is a healthcare issue and should be treated as such. This is clearly the case with our opioid epidemic.[35] We should not be throwing people in jail or prison over their addictions. **We must also ensure that those who are already in jail or prison over marijuana possession, use, or sales are granted clemency and set free.** We need to begin the work of healing our communities and our nation. The drug war should end.

---

[34] Ibid.

[35] Ibid.

Competition among businesses is essential to a free market.

Walmart's CEO recently called for a raise in the federal Minimum Wage.[36] Why would one of the leading employers in the country seek to increase its own labor costs? First, Walmart is competing in the market for labor. Walmart knows that it needs to offer competitive salaries in order to attract and retain employees. If Walmart doesn't pay living wages,

---

[36] Boyle, Matthew. "Walmart CEO Doug McMillon calls on Congress to boost federal minimum wage", 2019. Los Angeles Times. Accessed 19 July 2019. https://www.latimes.com/business/la-fi-walmart-congress-minimum-wage-20190605-story.html.

then some other company will be able to draw the employees away. This competition for labor helps to keep salaries at livable levels for the workers. Second, Walmart is competing with other retailers on selling retail items. If they take on higher costs from paying higher hourly rates to their workers, it will hurt their ability to compete on prices for the retail sales. The more they pay their workers, the more they'll have to charge for their products.

A minimum wage can help level the playing field in the market by ensuring no one business can gain an advantage by using cheap, underpaid labor. And so, a minimum wage helps to stabilize both the labor market and the retail market. With a high minimum wage, competitive advantage will be found in making superior products or increasing systemic efficiency. In turn, better-paid workers will be happier and will better contribute to the overall economy with their spending. **To encourage companies to compete on quality and avoid a race-to-the-bottom on labor salaries, the federal minimum wage should be $15 an hour and tied to inflation going forward.**

In addition to our minimum wage increase, we must end sub-minimum wage allowances for workers with disabilities. Current law allows states to grant exceptions to the minimum wage laws for companies that employ disabled workers. Some argue that this policy allows for workers with disabilities to get jobs that otherwise wouldn't exist. This is a weak argument that's used to attack all minimum wage laws. It fails here even more soundly as it is clearly not in the interest of a disabled worker to be underpaid. No one should be paid sub-minimum wages, and no companies should profit off of underpaying workers with disabilities.

***

The Americans with Disabilities Act (ADA) became law in 1990. The ADA is a civil rights law that prohibits discrimination against individuals with disabilities in all areas of public life, including jobs, schools, transportation, and all public and private places that are open to the general public. However, enforcement of these provisions in the business community has had some glaring holes throughout the nation. When businesses are unlikely to be sued for their ADA violations, a business that spends the money to follow the law is put at a competitive disadvantage from the companies that take their chances and break the law. **We must improve enforcement so that no business gets an unfair advantage by ignoring the law.** We must also ensure that builders and local planning departments aren't offloading the costs of compliance onto future businesses that will buy or lease their properties – the buildings should be made to code in the first place. Enforcement actions should occur at all levels. To ensure that internet businesses are also respecting civil rights for people with disabilities, we also need to codify and expand regulations made under the ADA to address accessibility online.[37]

***

When businesses cheat their customers, they're also cheating their honest competitors, cheating the market, and

---

[37] PDFs should have tags. Videos should have captions. When new technologies or modes of communication are being developed, disability should not be an afterthought; disability should be a primary concern.

hurting the economy. **Providing positive protection from liability, for companies that cheat, is antithetical to free market principles.**

For example, the Federal Arbitration Act has been abused by large companies to construct immunity from class action lawsuits. When those companies break the law, hurt consumers, and defraud the market, they face little or no consequences. This in turn encourages companies to break the law, creating an environment where the market suffers more and more. To ensure a competitive market, we must repeal or reform these federally-mandated provisions.

***

Monopolies and oligopolies are dangers to society.[38] We must work to improve our anti-trust regulation and enforcement to ensure that markets operate efficiently and effectively. A free market shouldn't mean that we hand the keys to the kingdom to a few giant corporations. If there's only one guy to buy from, it's not a market and it's not free.

Soon, Disney will be losing their copyright on Mickey Mouse.[39] That's the water-line, but it's not the flood. The flood

---

[38] See Schechter, Asher. "When Did Americans Stop Being Antimonopoly? Q&A with Richard R. John", 2016. Pro-Market. Accessed 19 July 2019. https://promarket.org/americans-stop-antimonopoly-q-richard-r-john/.

[39] See Lee, Timothy B. "Mickey Mouse will be public domain soon—here's what that means", 2019. ARS Technica. Accessed 19 July 2019. https://arstechnica.com/tech-policy/2019/01/a-whole-years-worth-of-works-just-fell-into-the-public-domain/.

is the millions of copyrighted ideas that should already be in the public domain. Their authors and creators are all dead and buried, but giant corporations continue to exert exclusive, government-backed control of the works and creations. Congress last extended copyright in 1998, and Disney has only become more powerful since then. No Republican should be for increasing the anti-market, government protections afforded under our current copyright scheme. What we really need is to reform copyright and bring it in-line with the Constitution's text: **Copyright should be "for limited times."** An unlimited copyright provided to a mega-corporation is unconstitutional and repugnant to a free market.

* * *

Americans understand that we need Net Neutrality legislation at the national level. And further, in order to create a real competitive internet-utility market, we need to reform the market by allowing for and providing for a public option to access the internet. Some states, including California, have made it illegal for cities and towns to build their own internet service for their residents. We need national legislation to combat this anti-free market approach and preempt these anti-competitive state laws.

* * *

Anti-trust laws help maintain a working market. But when talking about working-class people, their jobs searches are pretty competitive. If participation in a market is mandatory, then it can never really be a free market. And workers can't choose to go without a job. So, workers need equal-footing with their potential employers. One way to achieve that is through strong government regulation of workplace conditions, benefits, and pay. Another way to work a balance is to provide for strong Labor Unions. Both of these approaches usually work well together. **Anyone trying to sell you the lie that workplaces need neither government regulation nor collective bargaining is wrong.**

However, not all government regulation is good and not all unions act in the best interest of the workers. Some states have implemented Right to Work laws that outlaw "Shop Agreements" between unions and management that require the workers to pay the unions money even when they think the union is doing a bad job. Other states have provided protection for these agreements and insulation for a union's professional staff and board members. There is room for adjustment on both sides of this question.

We must provide for strong unions, and hold those unions accountable to the workers. **The American worker deserves everything they can bargain for.** And so, Congress should revise the National Labor Relations Act to bolster unions in our nation and protect collective bargaining rights, while providing funding and reforms for union elections, so that workers have a clear voice in how they are represented.

Universal healthcare is a moral imperative.

We are the wealthiest nation on Earth.[40] However, you wouldn't be able to tell that from looking at our healthcare system. The World Health Organization ranks our healthcare system at 37th among the world's nations.[41] America's healthcare system is the most expensive in the world but

---

[40] This is not only true when you measure by nominal Gross Domestic Product, but also when you look at our available land, resources, people, and future.

[41] Tandon, Ajay, et al. "Measuring Overall Health System Performance For 191 Countries." GPE Discussion Paper Series: No. 30. World Health Organization. Accessed July 19, 2019. https://www.who.int/healthinfo/paper30.pdf.

produces worse health outcomes than every other major country.[42]

***

We should replace our current for-profit, heavily regulated, and inefficient insurance system with a simpler system. Our healthcare system should be directly funded by tax dollars. This expansion of Medicare for all Americans would provide people access to their doctors without the need to purchase insurance, without paying premiums, and without copays. **No one should die in this nation because of a lack of money.** And no one should be made to pay their life savings to fight a disease.

Every other major country on Earth has some form of government-managed healthcare system. They each made this shift because they want to live longer, fuller lives. Americans deserve at least the care that other countries have.

Anyone insisting that a "free market" for healthcare would do a good job is ignoring the fact that we've tried and failed to make a working market for healthcare. **We tried it, it didn't work, let's move on to better, proven systems.** This should essentially be the Republican attitude on all our ventures – we have great thinkers, and we'll try their great ideas, and when the ideas fail, we'll move on to better ones. **The market is**

---

[42] See Davis, Karen & et al. Mirror, Mirror on the Wall. 2014. The Commonwealth Fund. Accessed 19 July 2019. https://www.commonwealthfund.org/sites/default/files/doc uments/___media_files_publications_fund_report_2014_jun_ 1755_davis_mirror_mirror_2014.pdf.

telling us we need a single-payer system; it'd be simply pig-headed to ignore it.

***

Going along with Medicare for All, we also need to take steps to better control prescription drug prices. Medicare should be given the power to bargain for drug prices, which it is forbidden to do under existing federal law.[43] We also need to ensure that drug research is well-funded and targeted towards curing disease. Patent protection helps encourage private research. But price gouging is a real problem,[44] and so patents should come with anti-gouging price controls.

***

A system of universal healthcare should include access to Reproductive Health services, including safe and legal abortions. Medicare should cover abortion services, just like it should cover any other necessary medical care. Women shouldn't be denied access to abortions just because they can't

---

[43] See Sanders, Bernie. "The Medicare Drug Price Negotiation Act of 2019, Background", 2019. U.S. Senate. Accessed 19 July 2019.
https://www.sanders.senate.gov/download/final_-medicare-drug-price-negotiation-act-of-2019—summary.

[44] See Chung, Andrew. "U.S. Top Court Rejects Maryland Bid to Revive Drug Price-Gouging Law", 2019. Reuters. Accessed 19 July 2019. https://www.reuters.com/article/us-usa-court-pharmaceuticals/us-top-court-rejects-maryland-bid-to-revive-drug-price-gouging-law-idUSKCN1Q81T9.

afford to pay for healthcare themselves. The Hyde Amendment, which currently limits federal funding for abortion services, should be repealed.

36

***

As part of our universal healthcare system, we must also require all hospitals to treat all patients, regardless of race, ethnicity, national origin, disability, age, religion, gender or transgender status, or sexual orientation. No hospital should be allowed to use the religious views of its board members, owners, or employees as an excuse to wrongfully discriminate against any American. If they want to own a hospital, run one, or work at one, then they must follow the law. **Freedom of religion means that everyone gets treated the same regardless of their religion; it does not mean you get to treat others poorly because of your religion.**

Public education is essential to a working democracy.

During his first campaign for the Illinois General Assembly, Abraham Lincoln's first political announcement on March 9, 1832, had this to say about education:

"Upon the subject of education, not presuming to dictate any plan or system respecting it, I can only say that I view it as the most important subject which we as a people can be engaged in. That every man may receive at least, a moderate education, and thereby be enabled to read the histories of his own and other countries, by which he may duly appreciate the value of our free institutions, appears to be an object of vital importance, even on this account alone, to say nothing of the advantages and satisfaction to be derived from all being able to read the scriptures and other works, both of a religious and moral nature, for themselves. For my part, I desire to see the time when education,

and by its means, morality, sobriety, enterprise and industry, shall become much more general than at present, and should be gratified to have it in my power to contribute something to the advancement of any measure which might have a tendency to accelerate the happy period." [45]

Today, while literacy is a focus of our education system, the horizon of a fully literate society is still pretty far away. It's estimated that only 13% of Americans can read at a high literacy level.[46] Another 50% of Americans have a basic reading level that allows them to comprehend short and medium-length texts, read news reports and stories, and understand simple charts and graphs.[47] But those same people may have difficulty critically analyzing information and news stories, making complex inferences, and understanding complex arguments.[48] The remaining 37% of Americans have a low-level of literacy.[49] However, most people understand the things they read most of the time.

When dealing with complex societal and governmental issues, the types of debates that drive elections and politics in our nation, our reluctance to read has led us to trust pundits,

---

[45] Lincoln, Abraham. First Political Announcement, 1832. Sangamo Journal. Accessed 24 July 2019. http://www.abrahamlincolnonline.org/lincoln/speeches/1832.htm

[46] Rampey, Bobby D., et al. "Skills of U.S. Unemployed, Young, and Older Adults in Sharper Focus", 2016. National Center for Education Statistics. Accessed 19 July 2019. https://nces.ed.gov/pubsearch/pubsinfo.asp?pubid=2016039rev. At page 10.

[47] Ibid. at 10.

[48] Ibid. at pg B-3.

[49] Ibid. at 10.

youtubers, and cable news channels to give us reliable information. However, there is a huge skill gap among Americans in the ability to critically assess news sources and media.[50] With foreign governments, huge corporations, and highly skilled operatives all trying to influence our democracy, we need a national effort to combat lies and misinformation. **Fake news is a national security threat that requires a national response.** We need national standards and curriculum to educate our youth about media literacy, and we need an education and outreach effort that reaches the adult population. **If a 10-year-old can learn the difference between fake and real news, then a 40-year-old should be able to learn it as well.**

***

Children as young as 4 years old should be provided with an education environment appropriate to their age and for preparation toward their future studies. Universal Pre-K should be provided for in every state in America. Being born poor should not give you fewer educational opportunities than someone born rich. People should be able to attain educational success based on merit, not the wealth they were born with. To that end, it shouldn't just be the well-off that send their kids to preschool.

---

[50] See Wineburg, Sam, et al. "Evaluating Information: The Cornerstone of Civic Online Reasoning", 2016. Stanford Digital Repository. Accessed 19 July 2019. https://purl.stanford.edu/fv751yt5934.

We should be a nation of lifetime learners. We need a national program for continuing education that provides access for rural and urban residents to continue learning about the world around them long after high school. We need to provide grants and stipends so that working adults can take time off of work to pursue education, not just to improve their working conditions and improve the American skillset, but to encourage more thoughtful participation in our society. **Learning new things shouldn't just be for young people or those desperate for higher incomes; it should be for everyone.** And while encouraging adult education, we should also ensure strong criminal enforcement against fraud and fake colleges designed to steal money from hard-working Americans. No one should be the victim of a fake-college-scam without redress from law enforcement. No one should defraud students without the fear of harsh prosecution looming over their illegal conduct.

Education reform is a complicated topic. "Reform" can be a scary word, used by people misrepresenting their own motives or the motives of others. However, while some "reformers" are seeking to eliminate public education entirely, others have bold ideas to improve public education. **We must always seek to improve education in our country.** To that end, we must pursue reforms ensuring that every public school in our nation is fully funded. **We don't build our highways on local property taxes alone, and we certainly shouldn't be**

building our education infrastructure on local property taxes alone.

***

In addition to reforms on inadequate funding models, we also need reforms on inadequate curriculum. The regiment of age-based education is not effective. Children, teenagers, and young adults should be treated like the individuals they are, provided tailored lessons to their level and to their personal rate of attainment. Their education should be based on what they know, how they learn, and how quickly they can move forward through their lessons; it shouldn't be based on arbitrary grade levels designed around progressing everyone of the same age at the same pace. **We all run at different speeds and we all learn at different speeds.** The way things are going now, we're holding some back from their potential while leaving others behind. We're treating most people like high school is a prison sentence instead of an opportunity to grow. With this in mind, we should make exit from high school a function of attainment and desire, not age.

A new emphasis should be placed on critical thinking, study of the humanities, logic and reasoning, and philosophy. **The morality of our country cannot be left to mere mathematicians and engineers.** Science, technology, engineering, and mathematics should all be taught with great vigor, but time, space, and funding should be made available to ensure those STEM students also know their world's history, the socioeconomic issues facing society, how to critically analyze information sources, and how to ensure our democracy continues to function.

***

Charter schools should be non-profit, transparent, accountable to parents, and temporary. **We need innovation, and charter schools provide one of many different paths for innovation.** However, the plan should always be to find the best model for our public school system. Charter schools are experiments that should run their course, be analyzed for their results, and then their resources should return to their parent districts. If a group of educators, parents, and students want to come together to show a better way of running a school, then we should give them that chance, and then we should take what they learn to apply it for everyone else.

***

Public colleges and universities should be tuition-free for everyone in America. One hundred years ago, we decided as a nation that high school should be free and compulsory. The rest of the world followed our lead, and now secondary education is considered standard among the world's nations. However, America isn't leading now. We have huge student debts, high tuition, and a majority of Americans unable to attend college.

One simple, affordable step that we can take is to fully fund our universities and colleges and ensure that everyone can get an education without taking on massive amounts of debt.

We must expand opportunities for voting, get money out of politics, and guarantee a right to vote to all Americans.

According to former Secretary of State Colin Powell,

"The Republican Party should be a party that says, 'We want everybody to vote,' and make it easier to vote and give them a reason to vote for the party." [51]

---

[51] Cirilli, Kevin. "Powell to GOP: End voter ID push", 2013. Politico. Accessed 19 July 2019.

It was President Dwight D. Eisenhower that first proposed civil rights legislation to address voter access for African American citizens in 1956,[52] 1957,[53] and throughout his presidency.[54] Eventually these Republican efforts, joined by Northern Democrats, would help bring about change at the national level through passage of the Civil Rights Act of 1964 and the Voting Rights Act of 1965. Both of these landmark pieces of legislation were passed with overwhelming Republican support in Congress.[55]

Since then, the Republican Party has joined with the Democratic Party to unanimously extend the provisions of the Voting Rights Act. However, far-right extremists and judicial activists have pushed to dismantle the act's protections, implement laws to suppress turnout, and enact political

---

https://www.politico.com/story/2013/01/colin-powell-republicans-voter-id-086488

[52] Eisenhower, Dwight D. State of the Union Address, 1956. https://www.infoplease.com/homework-help/us-documents/state-union-address-dwight-d-eisenhower-january-5-1956.

[53] See Eisenhower, Dwight D. State of the Union Address, 1957. https://www.infoplease.com/homework-help/us-documents/state-union-address-dwight-d-eisenhower-january-10-1957.

[54] See Eisenhower, Dwight D. State of the Union Address, 1961. https://www.infoplease.com/homework-help/us-documents/dwight-d-eisenhower-january-12-1961.

[55] See Jacobson, Louis. "Steele says GOP fought hard for civil rights bills in 1960s", 2010. Politifact. Accessed 19 July 2019. https://www.politifact.com/truth-o-meter/statements/2010/may/25/michael-steele/steele-says-gop-fought-hard-civil-rights-bills-196/.

gerrymandering schemes that seek to de-legitimize government.

***

If there's one cornerstone of democracy that everyone seems to agree with, it's that the one with the most votes should win the election. Gerrymandering works against this principle. Congress needs to pass federal anti-gerrymandering legislation. A party should get a majority of seats when they get a majority of the votes.

***

The Citizen's United ruling from the Supreme Court in 2010 has brought us to a new era of unlimited political spending. However, the problem of giant corporations interfering with our elections is not new. As President Eisenhower warned the American people in his farewell address in 1961:

"In the councils of government, we must guard against the acquisition of unwarranted influence, whether sought or unsought, by the military-industrial complex. The potential for the disastrous rise of misplaced power exists, and will persist." [56]

We must work to end the system of legalized bribery in our country. Campaign finance reform is a nonpartisan issue.

---

[56] See "Ike's Warning of Military Expansion, 50 Years Later", 2011. National Public Radio. Accessed 19 July 2019. https://www.npr.org/2011/01/17/132942244/ikes-warning-of-military-expansion-50-years-later.

As Senator John McCain had said in 2014, about the Supreme Court gutting our campaign finance regulations:

"We go through it historically: reform, corruption, reform, corruption... Right now, in my view, we're at the height of corruption, thanks to the United States Supreme Court." [57]

We must find legislative solutions to removing the influence of money from our politics. Public funding of elections should be a priority for any new campaign finance laws. We must also bring about better enforcement of anti-corruption laws, ensuring that the FBI is spending its resources investigating public corruption. If a government official takes a bribe, they should be investigated and arrested.

***

In addition to dismantling campaign finance laws, the Supreme Court has also rolled back voting rights protections. In 2013, the Supreme Court gutted the Voting Rights Act. And since then, the Court has only become more eager to strike down laws protecting voting rights.[58] Congress must do everything in its power to reinforce the Voting Rights Act. Congress should implement national automatic voter

---

[57] See Overby, Peter. "McCain Made Campaign Finance Reform A Years-Long Mission", 2018. National Public Radio. Accessed 19 July 2019. https://www.npr.org/2018/08/26/572693293/mccain-made-campaign-finance-reform-a-years-long-mission.

[58] See Savage, David G.; Barabak, Mark Z. "Supreme Court's Approval of Partisan Gerrymandering Raises 2020 Election Stakes", 2019. Los Angeles Times. Accessed 19 July 2019. https://www.latimes.com/politics/la-na-pol-supreme-court-partisan-gerrymandering-republicans-20190627-story.html.

registration, requirements for early voting, and independent redistricting committees.

***

The security of our elections is a priority concern. We must do all we can to prevent cyber intrusions into our elections systems. This means that as a nation, we must set high standards for Voting Equipment security, provide for continuing funds to ensure we always have the most-up-to-date voting systems, and provide for inspections, auditing, and cooperation at a national level. But on balance, we must also ensure access and accessibility. An elections system that loses 60% of the votes to apathy, inconvenience, voter suppression, and inaccessibility, is not a secure elections system.

***

The right to vote is the right that's protective of all other rights. With that in mind, the right to vote should be enshrined in a new constitutional amendment, granting Congress clear powers to regulate elections nationwide, reversing the rulings in Citizen's United and Shelby County. Passage of a voting rights amendment should be the priority of every state legislature and every member of Congress that believes in freedom and democracy.

It is our duty to teach good civic engagement to our children.

To ensure our democracy continues to function, it's not enough just to vote on Election Day. We must get involved, continuously, in our communities and our government.

One hundred years ago, most states didn't allow women to vote. The push for women's rights didn't start in the halls of Congress, in the White House, or at the Supreme Court. It started in community meetings and with women and men going door to door and person to person. Community organizing is an essential feature of our democratic system.

The First Amendment protects the freedom of speech in our country. But that freedom is wasted on giant corporations, allowing them to buy and sell political opinions. We need a real, grassroots political revolution in our country. We need people talking directly to each other about the issues that matter to them. The First Amendment guarantees the right of each of us to knock on our neighbor's door and talk to them about our community, our society, and our government.

***

Counties, cities, towns, and other forms of local government are some of the ways that we cooperate as fellow citizens. Most people aren't even aware of the local laws that they live by and that effect their lives. But those local governments have elected officials that we can talk to and open meetings that we can attend. We must make an effort to take part in our local affairs.

***

Today, administrative agencies exist at all levels of our government. Both State and Federal agencies have the power to enact rules and regulations that carry the force of law. Each of these agencies give public notice and provide for public comment on potential regulations. While there are too many issues for each of us to give our opinions on all of them, there must be at least one topic for each of us to care about. Whether the things we care about are the rules that regulate the industry that we work in or the business that we manage, or the rules that effect our homes and our schools, we should seek to be informed. And we should try to influence how our government operates. Everyone, from the truck unloader to the investment banker, has a valuable opinion to give their government.

***

State laws passed by state legislatures have a huge impact on all of our lives. But most people don't even know who their state legislator is, what bills they are voting for, or how their state government is being run. People rely on news stories, television, and social media posts for all their information about the government. We can do better. We can promise that our children will know who their mayor is, who their state legislators are, and why those positions matter.

***

One way that we engage with each other and the government is through Political Parties. Parties help us sort through all of the complexities in politics. They also give us a team to root for. We have a duty to shape our political parties to be forces for good. We should have allegiance to each other, to our ideals, and to our belief in a better tomorrow. But we shouldn't accept whatever our leaders say just because they're on our team. We should hold our party leaders accountable, challenge them to come up with better ideas than they had yesterday, and replace them with new leaders if they fall short or fall behind.

***

If we can ensure that the next generation of adults are well-informed, curious, critical thinkers, then our country will be in safe hands. That should be our goal.

Index

www.ingramcontent.com/pod-product-compliance
Lightning Source LLC
Chambersburg PA
CBHW072341270726
48659CB00022B/2117